EASY MAGIC TRICKS

COOL CARD TRICKS

by Steve Charney

CAPSTONE PRESS
a capstone imprint

First Facts is published by Capstone Press,
151 Good Counsel Drive, P.O. Box 669, Mankato, Minnesota 56002.
www.capstonepub.com

 Books published by Capstone Press are manufactured with paper
containing at least 10 percent post-consumer waste.

Library of Congress Cataloging-in-Publication Data
Charney, Steve.
  Cool card tricks / by Steve Charney.
    p. cm. — (First facts. Easy magic tricks)
  Includes bibliographical references and index.
  Summary: "Step-by-step instructions and photos describe how to perform
magic card tricks"—Provided by publisher.
  ISBN 978-1-4296-4515-7 (library binding)
  1. Card tricks—Juvenile literature. I. Title. II. Series.
  GV1549.C48 2011
  793.8'5—dc22   2009048835

5661

Editorial Credits
Kathryn Clay, editor; Matt Bruning, designer; Marcy Morin, scheduler;
  Sarah Schuette, photo stylist; Eric Manske, production specialist

Photo Credits
All photos by Capstone Press/Karon Dubke, except Ed Hord, 24

Printed in the United States of America in North Mankato, Minnesota.
012011   006047R

TABLE OF CONTENTS

INTRODUCTION

Welcome to the world of magic! Are you ready to become a **magician**? Well, you've come to the right place. There are plenty of fun and easy magic tricks to perform. Here are eight simple card tricks to get you started.

Doing a trick well takes practice. Before doing these tricks for your family, friends, or pet gorilla, practice them. Once you've mastered the trick, you're ready for an **audience**.

Grab a deck of cards. Then get ready to amaze your family and friends.

magician—a person who performs magic tricks
audience—people who watch or listen to a play, movie, or show

MAGIC TIP

Magicians never tell how the tricks are done. Here's why:

1 You can never do the trick again for the same audience.

2 The audience might be disappointed by how simple the trick is.

3 Other magicians could catch you telling their secrets. They might try to saw you in half!

FLIP-FLOP

Your friend will "flip" when her card is found **face** down in the deck.

• • • Getting Ready:

Secretly flip the bottom card in a deck face up.

• • • The Trick:

1

Have a friend pick a card. Don't let her see the bottom card.

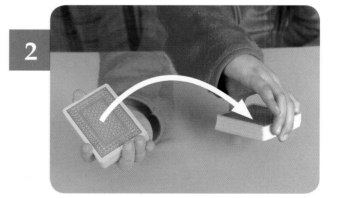

2

While she looks at her card, quickly turn over the deck.

face—the side of the card that shows the number or kind

3 Have her put the card into the deck face down. Don't **fan** the cards or she'll see the other cards facing up.

4 Cover the cards with a scarf. Flip over the top card.

5 Say some magic words. Take off the scarf and fan the cards. Your friend's card is face down!

MAGIC TIP

Everyone knows "Abracadabra." Try making up new magic words like "Flippity Floppity."

fan—spread the cards apart so each one can be seen

BUBBLE CARDS

Make cards rise to the top of the deck like bubbles. The cards are not the same. But your dad will think they are.

• • • • • • **Getting Ready:**

Find the 7 of hearts and the 8 of diamonds. Put them face down on top of the deck.

Next, find the 7 of diamonds and the 8 of hearts. Hold them in your hand face up.

The Trick:

1 Show the two cards in your hand. Put them into the middle of the deck.

2 Say, "Some cards rise like bubbles."

3 Tap the deck and turn over the top two cards. Take your bow.

MAGIC TIP

Don't show the cards too fast or too slow. People might catch on to the trick.

THE KEY CARD

Magicians can find any card in a deck.
They just need to know what to look for.

Getting Ready:

Look at the bottom
card of a deck. This
is your key card.
Don't forget it!

The Trick:

1

Have your friend pick a card.
Put her card on top of the deck.

Cut the deck two or three times.

Fan the deck toward you. Look for the key card. Your friend's card will be to the right of it.

Put the card face down on the table. Ask your friend what card she picked.

Turn over her card. Ta-da!

cut—to divide a deck into two parts; put the bottom part on the top part

MAGIC FINGERS

Did you know you could guess a card just by feeling it? You can if you're a magician!

Getting Ready:

Cut a small hole in a bottom corner of a paper lunch bag.

The Trick:

1

Shuffle the cards.

shuffle—to mix up a deck of cards

2

Say, "A magician has magic fingers. Watch!" Put the cards into the bag. Don't let anyone see the hole.

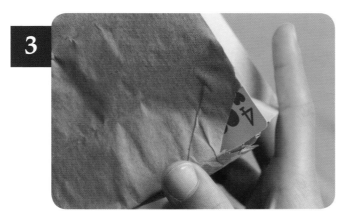

3

Hold the bag up. Then find the bottom card. Move it near the hole. Secretly take a look.

4

With your hand in the bag, tell your friend what card you're holding. Take out the card and show it to him. Repeat the trick with a different card.

MAGIC TIP

Keep the hole facing you, and hold the bag high. Look at the card quickly. This way no one will think something is fishy.

TWO PILES, ONE CARD

It's easy to find your mom's card in a pile.
Just look for the one that's different.

Getting Ready:

Secretly divide the cards into two piles by color.

The Trick:

1

Put the two piles face down in front of you.

2 Ask your mom to pick a card from one pile. Have her put it into the second pile.

3 Shuffle the second pile.

4 Look for her card. It will be the only one that is a different color.

5 Show her the card and take a bow.

ACES ON TOP

Magicians are known for making things disappear. But sometimes the trick is making things appear. Watch as the aces suddenly show up on top.

Getting Ready:

Secretly put the four aces face down on top of the deck.

The Trick:

1

Separate the deck into four equal piles. The four aces will be on top of the first pile.

2

Pick up the last pile. Move the top three cards to the bottom.

Then put one card from the top onto each of the other three piles.

3

Repeat step 2 with the other three piles.

4

Turn over the top card of each pile. The four aces are magically on top.

THE FOUR PIRATES

Pirates are sneaky. Watch them escape by magically rising to the top of the deck.

• • • • • **Getting Ready:**

Pull out the four jacks. Place three other cards on top of the jacks.

• • • • • **The Trick:**

1

Fan out the jacks face up. The three secret cards should be hidden behind them.

2

Say, "Four pirates robbed a bank." Put the cards on top of the deck face down.

3

Say, "One pirate went to the third floor." Take the top card and put it in the deck near the top.

4

Say, "Another pirate went to the second floor." Take the next card and put it in the middle of the deck.

5

Say, "A third pirate went to the first floor." Put the card near the bottom of the deck.

6

Say, "The last pirate waited on the roof." Show the top card and put it back.

7

Say, "He heard sirens and warned his friends." Hit the cards three times.

8

Turn over the top four cards. Say, "The pirates ran away."

FINGERPRINTS

It's easy to find your friend's card.
Just look for his fingerprints.

Getting Ready:

Look at the bottom card of a
deck. This is your key card.
Don't forget it!

The Trick:

1

Have your friend pick a
card. Put the card on top
of the deck face down.

2

Cut the deck two or
three times.

Say, "I can find your card by the fingerprints you left." Look at your friend's fingers. Pretend to **memorize** his fingerprints.

Fan the deck toward you. Look for the key card. Your friend's card will be to the right of it.

Pick up his card. Look at it closely. Say, "This card has your fingerprints all over it!"

memorize—to remember something

GLOSSARY

audience (AW-dee-uhns)—people who watch or listen to a play, movie, or show

cut (CUT)—to divide a deck into two parts; put the bottom part on the top part

face (FAYSE)—the side of the card that shows the number or kind

fan (FAHN)—to hold the deck with both hands and spread the cards apart so each one can be seen

fingerprint (FING-gur-print)—the pattern made by the curved ridges on the tips of your fingers

key card (KEE CARD)—the card to look for when finding someone's card; the person's card will always be to the right of the key card

magician (ma-JI-shuhn)—a person who performs magic tricks

memorize (MEM-uh-rize)—to remember something

perform (pur-FORM)—to give a show in public

shuffle (SHUHF-uhl)—to mix up a deck of cards

READ MORE

Charney, Steve. *Hocus-Jokus: How to Do Funny Magic*. Minnetonka, Minn.: Meadowbrook Press, 2003.

Fullman, Joe. *Card Tricks*. Magic Handbook. Laguna Hills, Calif.: QEB Publishing, 2008.

Ho, Oliver. *Young Magician: Card and Magic Tricks*. New York: Main Street, 2005.

INTERNET SITES

FactHound offers a safe, fun way to find Internet sites related to this book. All of the sites on FactHound have been researched by our staff.

Here's all you do:

Visit *www.facthound.com*

Type in this code: 9781429645157

INDEX

ABOUT THE AUTHOR

Steve Charney learned magic when he was a little kid. Now he performs more than 100 times each year.

Steve is also a ventriloquist, radio personality, musician, and songwriter. He has written songbooks, storybooks, joke books, and magic books. Look for his performances on the Internet.